SCOTNOTES
Number 19

Naomi Mitchison's *Early in Orcadia, The Big House* and *Travel Light*

Moira Burgess

Association for Scottish Literary Studies 2004

Acknowledgements
I would like to thank the Association for Scottish Literary Studies Schools and Further Education Committee for their wise scrutiny of this work, and especially Ronald Renton, Convener of the committee, for his generous assistance, and the President of the ASLS, Alan MacGillivray, for his strong and subtle hand in guiding the original conception of this study-note. I am also particularly grateful to Julie Renfrew of St Margaret's Academy, Livingston, who kindly and helpfully read and commented on earlier drafts.

Published by
Association for Scottish Literary Studies
c/o Department of Scottish History
University of Glasgow
9 University Gardens
Glasgow G12 8QH
www.asls.org.uk

First published 2004

© Moira Burgess

A CIP catalogue for this title is available from the British Library

ISBN 0 948877 61 8

Subsidised by

Printed in Great Britain by Bell and Bain Ltd, Glasgow

Typeset by Roger Booth Associates, Hassocks, West Sussex

CONTENTS

                                                       Page

Naomi Mitchison: life and work 1

Early in Orcadia 5
The story/stories of the novel
Theme and structure of the novel
Setting in geography and prehistory
Characters
Language
Myth and religion

The Big House 18
The story of the novel
Theme and structure of the novel
Characters
Setting and language
Historical periods
Celtic myths and folklore

Travel Light 30
The story of the novel
The structure of the novel
Characters
Setting in time and place
Themes
Norse myths and legends

Conclusion 40

Bibliography 41

SCOTNOTES

Study guides to major Scottish writers and literary texts

Produced by the Schools and Further Education Committee
of the Association for Scottish Literary Studies

Series Editors
Lorna Borrowman Smith
Ronald Renton

Editorial Board
Ronald Renton, St Aloysius' College, Glasgow
(Convener, Schools and Further Education Committee, ASLS)
William Aitken, Stevenson College, Edinburgh
Jim Alison, HMI (retired)
Dr Eleanor Bell, University of Strathclyde
Dr Morna Fleming, Beath High School, Cowdenbeath
Professor Douglas Gifford, University of Glasgow
John Hodgart, Garnock Academy, Kilbirnie
Alan Keay, Portobello High School. Edinburgh
Alan MacGillivray, University of Strathclyde
Dr James McGonigal, University of Glasgow
Rev Jan Mathieson, The Manse, Croy, Inverness
Lorna Ramsay, Fairlie, Ayrshire
Dr Kenneth Simpson, University of Strathclyde
Lorna Borrowman Smith, Wallace High School, Stirling

THE ASSOCIATION FOR SCOTTISH LITERARY STUDIES aims to promote the study, teaching and writing of Scottish literature, and to further the study of the languages of Scotland.

To these ends, the ASLS publishes works of Scottish literature; literary criticism and in-depth reviews of Scottish books in *Scottish Studies Review*; short articles, features and news in *ScotLit*; and scholarly studies of language in *Scottish Language*. It also publishes *New Writing Scotland*, an annual anthology of new poetry, drama and short fiction, in Scots, English and Gaelic. ASLS has also prepared a range of teaching materials covering Scottish language and literature for use in schools.

All the above publications are available as a single 'package', in return for an annual subscription. Enquiries should be sent to: ASLS, c/o Department of Scottish History, 9 University Gardens, University of Glasgow, Glasgow G12 8QH. Telephone/fax +44 (0)141 330 5309, e-mail d.jones@scothist.arts.gla.ac.uk or visit our website at **www.asls.org.uk**

EDITOR'S FOREWORD

The *Scotnotes* booklets are a series of study guides to major Scottish writers and literary texts that are likely to be elements within literature courses. They are aimed at senior pupils in secondary schools and students in further education colleges and colleges of education. Each booklet in the series is written by a person who is not only an authority on the particular writer or text but also experienced in teaching at the relevant levels in schools or colleges. Furthermore, the editorial board, composed of members of the Schools and Further Education Committee of the Association for Scottish Literary Studies, considers the suitability of each booklet for the students in question.

For many years there has been a shortage of readily accessible critical notes for the general student of Scottish literature. *Scotnotes* has grown as a series to meet this need, and provides students with valuable aids to the understanding and appreciation of the key writers and major texts within the Scottish literary tradition.

Lorna Borrowman Smith
Ronald Renton

NOTE ON REFERENCES
Page references are to the following
editions of the works discussed:
Early in Orcadia, House of Lochar, 2000.
The Big House, Canongate Kelpies, 1987.
Travel Light, Virago, 1985

1. Naomi Mitchison: life and work

Naomi Mitchison was born Naomi Haldane in Edinburgh on 1 November 1897, and spent her childhood in Oxford, where her father, the physiologist J.S. Haldane, held a fellowship at New College. Her brother, J.B.S. Haldane, became a distinguished geneticist, and her early interests too were scientific, but she was a highly imaginative child, given to making up stories for herself, a pointer perhaps to her later career. She was educated at the Dragon School in Oxford and then by a governess at home. She studied science as a home student of St Anne's College for a year, but did not take a degree.

She married Gilbert Richard (Dick) Mitchison in 1916 and they set up home in London, where Dick practised as a barrister; he later became a Member of Parliament, and was created Lord Mitchison in 1965, though Naomi herself seldom used her title. Their marriage lasted until Dick's death in 1970. For many years it was an open marriage, with lovers known and accepted on both sides. They had seven children, of whom five survived to adulthood.

Mitchison's upbringing and life before 1920 had largely proceeded on conventional upper-middle-class lines, though from an early age, thanks to her father's position, she was in contact with the intellectual world to an unusual degree. In the 1920s she began to break out of her expected role of wife and mother, developing interests in social problems and politics which she retained throughout her life. In politics she was a socialist, later a supporter of Scottish nationalism, but above all an internationalist; she began at this time the travelling which was to take her all over the world. All her life, too, she supported women's causes: most of her novels have independent feminist heroines, many of them not unlike herself.

She now began a writing career which would cover more than sixty years and produce close on a hundred books – novels, non-fiction and children's books – together with a vast amount of shorter writing: short stories, poems and journalism. It was her husband Dick who introduced her to classical history, which she began to read eagerly, and her first novel, *The Conquered* (1923), is set in Gaul during Roman times. Her historical novels are based on exhaustive research. Her characters, however, come to life through the use of colloquial, slangy dialogue, now slightly dated perhaps, but original and fresh at the time.

The novels and short story collections she published over the next ten years were both popular and critically acclaimed. This phase of her writing culminated in the epic novel *The Corn King and the Spring Queen* (1931), set in the fictional country of Marob and in historical Sparta and Egypt in the first and second centuries BC.

Like most people in the 1930s, she was worried about the political situation in Europe, where the rise of the Nazi movement was threatening another world war. Mitchison visited the Soviet Union in 1932 and Austria in 1934, observing what was happening and where possible speaking to ordinary people to get all points of view. Meanwhile she was writing her first novel with a modern setting, *We Have Been Warned*, which draws on her Soviet visit and her fears about the future. Unusually in her career so far, she had difficulty in getting it published, not because of the politics but because of some scenes which were considered too sexually explicit at the time. It was eventually published in 1935, but was not well received by critics, and for the first time Mitchison found herself slightly marginalised on the London literary scene.

In 1937 the Mitchisons bought Carradale House in Kintyre, south Argyll, originally as a holiday home and a safe retreat for the family in the event of war. When World War II did break out in September 1939, Mitchison was living there with her two youngest children, and Carradale became her home for the rest of her life, the focus of her extended family and a base for her travels. She spent the war running the big house and its farm and trying to build a relationship with the villagers, while often aware of her own loneliness and the potential danger to Dick, who had stayed in London. The extracts from her war diary published in 1985 as *Among You Taking Notes* give an unforgettable picture of these difficult years.

She had little time for writing, but worked when she could on her next novel, *The Bull Calves*, published in 1947. It is set in the house of Gleneagles, a Haldane family home, in 1747, not long after the battle of Culloden. The story of Kirstie Haldane and her husband, Lowland and Highland in a mutually rewarding relationship, is used by Mitchison to symbolise her hopes for a Scotland which in 1947 was recovering from World War II, as the Scotland of the novel is recovering from the stresses of the Jacobite risings. She was now settled in the West Highlands and the area provides a background for several of her novels at this time, such as the children's fantasy *The Big House* (1950) and the social comedy *Lobsters on the Agenda* (1952). The collection of short stories and poems *Five Men and a Swan* (1957) contains some of her finest work from this period.

Her writing in the 1950s otherwise covers several fronts. An enthusiasm for the Norse sagas contributed to the fantasy *Travel Light* (1952) and several books on the Vikings. A long-standing interest in Arthurian legends led to the highly original *To the Chapel Perilous* (1955), in which newspaper reporters with thoroughly twentieth-century attitudes report on the quest for the Holy Grail. She published a number of children's books in the 1950s and early 1960s, though there was also a significant development in her adult fiction with the publication of *Memoirs of a Spacewoman* (1962), a feminist science fiction novel still highly regarded in its field. She continued to write science fiction novels and short stories throughout her career.

The early 1960s, however, saw a major change in her life. She befriended a young African who was studying in Britain, and became deeply involved in the life of his tribe and village in Botswana. She visited him there, attended his installation as chief of the Bakgatla tribe, and from then on spent part of each year in Botswana, herself becoming acknowledged as Mmarona or mother of the tribe. Several novels arose from this engagement with Africa, the first being *When We Become Men* (1965). In 1966 she published a memoir of her first years there, *Return to the Fairy Hill*.

During the 1970s she published three invaluable memoirs of her childhood, adolescence and early married life, *Small Talk* (1973), *All Change Here* (1975), and *You May Well Ask* (1979). A selection of her poems, *The Cleansing of the Knife*, appeared in 1978, and some of her many short stories were collected in *Images of Africa* (1980), *What Do You Think Yourself?* (1982), and *A Girl Must Live* (1990). Her work was beginning to receive critical attention, and short fiction from earlier in her career was reprinted in *Beyond This Limit* (1985).

Perhaps the most impressive of her late work – it was published when she was nearly ninety years old – is *Early in Orcadia* (1987). She returned to the historical fiction with which her career began, but went much farther back, in fact to prehistoric times, attempting with much success to recreate the life of the first settlers in Orkney three or four thousand years BC.

Naomi Mitchison died in Carradale at the age of 101 on 11 January 1999. Though she has always been acknowledged as a significant Scottish writer, her work has perhaps at times not been fully valued. Criticism and research are now beginning to reveal her skill and originality, and also the breadth of knowledge, sympathy and understanding to be found in both her writing and her life.

2. Early in Orcadia (1987)

Early in Orcadia is a novel, or a story sequence (see later, **Theme and structure of the novel**), set in Stone Age Orkney, about 3000 BC. Naomi Mitchison had begun her career, over sixty years before, by writing historical novels, but she did not usually choose a period quite so far in the past, and by doing so here she sets herself a number of problems.

A good deal is known or can be surmised from archaeological investigations about how Stone Age people lived, what they ate, how they hunted or farmed. That part of the writing would present no great difficulty to a writer skilled in research and its use in fiction. (Mitchison is particularly good at this: you could probably make and fire a clay pot, or cook meat the Neolithic way, from the details she gives.) Much more problematic are the people themselves, the characters which a novel must have. Since we cannot know how they talked, how is the writer to convey what they say and how they say it? Behind that question is the really big one: how did they think? What did they suppose made the sun rise and set, the moon wax and wane? What did they think about birth and death, major events in their lives as in ours? What, if anything, did they think happened before birth and after death?

Mitchison confronts all these problems in *Early in Orcadia*. She admits she is sometimes guessing, but usually she is basing her guesses on a guiding principle which lies behind much of her work. 'There is no reason to suppose,' she writes, 'that men and women then were totally different from men and women now.' (p. 5).

The story/stories of the novel
Mitchison probably intends us to consider *Early in Orcadia* as one story in several episodes (see later, **Theme and structure of the novel**). However, since each episode has a different central character and there is a gap of several generations between one episode and the next, it may be useful to look at them first as five separate stories, before investigating how and why Mitchison links them together.

1. The Hands and Metoo story: exploration and settlement (pp. 9-84)
In a Stone Age village on the north coast of Scotland, a wise old man studies the sea from a clifftop, seeing the patterns of a regular movement in the water which could perhaps be used to carry a boat out and back. He sees a shining far away which

seems to be a wonderful place beyond the sea. He is too old to pursue his ideas, but explains them to his son Hands.

Hands builds a boat and sails off with his wife Metoo, their baby, his older son and daughter and two other boys, taking seed corn, lambs, calves, fishing gear and bows and arrows. As the old man had worked out, the currents help them to cross to the Shining. One boy is drowned, but the others land safely, discovering that the Shining is only another piece of land. They build a house and plant corn. They are joined by a woman who reached the Shining some years before. Her companions have died, and she dies in childbirth, but her children join the family group.

Next spring Hands and his son sail back on a visit to the mainland, leaving Metoo in charge of the animals and crops. His stories interest some of the villagers and another man begins to build a boat. Hands returns to Metoo with the news that more people are on the way; they will help each other, share skills, and build up their settlement.

2. *The Little Honey story: art and craftsmanship (pp. 91-110)*
Little Honey's mother is a potter, one of an honoured group of women in the tribe. The skills of the potter women are passed on to their daughters and it is time for Little Honey to begin her apprenticeship. She makes a special pot, her first, and is distressed to find that it must be given to the eagles who are the tribal totem. She is taken to the priestess, the Big Woman or Good Woman. Reluctantly she follows the ritual, but after her initiation she decides it has been worth while: she now possesses the skill and creative power of a potter, an artist.

3. *The Pigsie story: storytelling (pp. 117-132)*
The young man Pigsie is kept hard at work carrying stones to build the great tomb where the bones of the dead are protected by the eagles and the ancestors of the tribe. Strangers come to view the bones and Pigsie's sister marries one of them: an important part of the ceremony is a visit to the tomb and a ritual by which the future of their coming baby is foretold. Pigsie has the gift of storytelling; later he becomes well-known for it and attains a life of leisure, honoured as the storyteller of the tribe.

4. *The Third-boy and the Other story: us and them (pp. 140-152)*
Third-boy has killed a deer, which is good, but he may also have killed a stranger, whom he thinks of as the Other, which is bad.

Early in Orcadia

The wise Old Ones of his tribe go with him to find the Other, who is not badly injured and recovers. The Old Ones can speak his language; they teach Third-boy a few words and he learns how to call the stranger his brother.

The people of the tribe have only fragmentary knowledge and wild rumours about the Others. When Third-boy brings the Other home, they see that he is different in some ways but a person like themselves. Later, the Other takes Third-boy back to his home.

5. *The Moon Woman story: astronomy and religion (pp. 161-176)*

The men have gone from the Eagle settlement, possibly (the women think) to learn how to measure time by the sun. Their own Moon Woman knows all about the moon and tides. One of the men returns with strangers who want the Moon Woman to go back with them; they honour her for her knowledge, and need her help because their own Moon Woman has died before telling them a certain vital secret.

Moon Woman goes with them to a place ruled by a Sun Man, where great standing stones have been raised to track the sun. She is asked to calculate when there will next be a solar eclipse, a significant event for the tribe, and begins to work it out from her observations of sun and moon. Meanwhile she observes the powerful Sun Man, and considers making love to him, so that they will be sun and moon together.

Theme and structure of the novel

As we have seen, *Early in Orcadia* consists of five stories, set hundreds of years apart in time and dealing with different characters, but connected by their location in a particular corner of Orkney during the period known as the Stone Age. Mitchison links them formally by interpolating passages of fact and explanation between the fictional episodes, and speculating in her own voice about what happened in prehistory, as far as it can be known from archaeological research, and how it fits in with the world of today. Some readers may find this a little disconcerting and feel that the loose structure of stories and commentary makes for a clumsy book.

However, this is part of Mitchison's plan. The slightly awkward jumps from one story to the next indicate that the development of the human race was not a completely smooth and seamless process. There must have been significant moments when a highly important discovery or invention took place. (We may think of the invention of the wheel at some unknown date, or – in modern times – the discovery of the double helix of DNA.) Mitchison is giving us imaginary snapshots of the prehistoric world at or just after such moments: the discovery of ocean currents, the realisation that people from another tribe are human like ourselves.

Yet each discovery blends into the continuing stream of life, and Mitchison demonstrates that too. In the linking passages, speaking openly as the author, she makes a point of telling us what happens to her fictional characters after the end of their particular episode. Metoo lives into a wise and respected old age (p. 86). Little Honey makes more and better pots (p. 112). Gradually these continuations of the fictional episodes extend farther into the factual commentary, until the last of the linking passages is nearly all fiction, containing the end of the Third-boy story (pp. 154-156) and a prequel to the story of Moon Woman and Sun Man (pp. 158-160). Fact and fiction have merged, the episodes are scarcely separated at all, and this is Mitchison's intention. The structure of *Early in Orcadia* is demonstrating its theme: that there are sudden advances but just one story running from the earliest times to the present day, and it is the story of humankind.

As different episodes focus on different human abilities and ideas – art, storytelling, understanding of others – we can see, over the novel, how each makes its contribution to the whole. Hands has reached the Shining, but he can see another Shining back where he has come from: that puzzles him, and he tries to work it out. Metoo makes a tentative experiment at weaving threads of wool together, something no one she knows has ever done before. Third-boy's tribe cannot believe that Others are real people: in their world, they themselves are the only people who exist. But by the last episode Moon Woman goes confidently to a strange place, admires the beautiful woven cloths, co-operates with the people of another tribe. Episode by episode, humankind has moved on.

Setting in place and prehistory
In her introduction (pp. 5-8) Naomi Mitchison gives us a glimpse of the earliest inspiration for the novel: the sight of the 'shining white line of Orkney' (p. 8) from the north coast of Scotland, looking across the Pentland Firth. 'That stayed with me,' says Mitchison (p. 8), and it is one of the first images in the novel, the bright 'something' beyond the sea, which in the minds of Mitchison's characters becomes the Shining. With her novelist's

imagination Mitchison realises that, though so much has changed, she has seen something which would have been the same in their time as in hers.

Long after this first glimmer of an idea, she visited the Tomb of the Eagles on the island of South Ronaldsay, one of the most mysterious and fascinating of Orkney's many prehistoric monuments, and this was the major stimulus for the novel. Though Mitchison does not specify the site of the first landfall, she has probably imagined Hands and Metoo landing on what is now South Ronaldsay; it is the southernmost of the Orkney islands, the first land they would come to. Certainly it is the setting for the later episodes, when 'the old ones ... sit in the open space where the flat stones get warm in the sun, their back to the great, honoured bone-place.' (p. 148) That is an exact description of the clifftop site of the Tomb of the Eagles: it is more officially known as the chambered tomb of Isbister, and can still be seen today.

In the last episode Moon Woman travels by boat from the home of the Eagle tribe to another place where 'on the ridge of the land there was something that could not be, standing against the sky, tall and dark grey. Many of them. Taller than two men. Than three men.' (p. 167) Mitchison probably means us to understand that Moon Woman is looking at the standing stones in the great Ring of Brodgar, a henge monument (think of Stonehenge: Brodgar is just as old and just as impressive) in the west of the main island of Orkney. Like the Tomb of the Eagles, it can still be seen and retains an atmosphere of immense mystery and power.

Mitchison's dating of events, at first glance, does not seem to be very precise: 'a very long time ago, some five or six thousand years back'. (p. 5) In fact this is carefully placed. 'Five or six thousand years back' from the 1980s, when she was writing *Early in Orcadia*, is around 3000-4000 BC. When she wrote, improved carbon dating had quite recently shown that settlement in Orkney began around 3500 BC, and the building of the Tomb of the Eagles had similarly been put at around 3150 BC. The Ring of Brodgar probably took many years to build, perhaps also in the second or third millennium BC.

As we have seen, *Early in Orcadia* consists of a number of episodes covering a fairly long period of time. Mitchison does not specify how much time passes between episodes, but by the last one, though the Tomb of the Eagles is still in use and standing stones are still being raised, one of the characters has a knife of 'the new stuff' (p. 169), not stone. We are to understand that the

Bronze Age is at hand. It is about 2000 BC and the events of *Early in Orcadia* have covered some 1500 years.

In writing all her historical fiction – in this case, prehistorical – Mitchison carries out exhaustive research, but she is ready to go beyond the strict bounds of archaeological proof. Though it is true that, when the Tomb of the Eagles was excavated, bones of sea eagles were found mixed with the human remains, Mitchison explains that her version of what happened there is only one of several possible interpretations. Similarly it is true that many of the ancient monuments in Orkney seem to be sited with reference to positions of the sun and moon at specific times of year. Mitchison builds on this in the last episode, following a slightly controversial theory (see later, **Myth and religion**), to suggest why this might be so and how the sites were used. She is perfectly frank about her methods: 'Probably it wasn't like that at all. But yet perhaps it was.'

This points up what she has done in *Early in Orcadia*, something that only a novelist can do. This is not an archaeological textbook. It is not just that the information she has gained by research provides a background for her characters. Rather, she has thought herself into their time and into their minds. She knows about the Tomb of the Eagles from books and site visits, but they know more about it, because it is part of their lives.

Characters

Since the episodes of *Early in Orcadia* are several generations apart in time, each naturally deals with a different group of people, but in each we can pick out one or two central characters. In some cases the central character is little more than a showcase for the particular human ability or concept on which that episode focuses. We know nothing about Third-boy, for instance, beyond the fact that after nearly killing a stranger he learns to treat him as a brother. The lively if rather irritating Pigsie is a budding storyteller and nothing more. His sister Ba's alliance with a boy from the Stick tribe is there purely to introduce the Tomb of the Eagles and its central place in the life of the community. In these episodes Mitchison carries out her intention of illustrating a phase of prehistoric life, but the characters are some way short of being fully developed.

From her preface, however, it is clear that she is interested in the Stone Age people as people, as men and women not unlike ourselves, and some of her characters are explored much more fully, as a fictional character should be. 'I am almost sure,' she writes,

Early in Orcadia

'that we, today, underestimate the intelligence, ingenuity and perhaps goodness, of our remote ancestors.' (p. 8) Hands in the first episode, one of the most remote of the ancestors she depicts, is intelligent, ingenious and good. His name indicates the manual skill and dexterity for which he is known, but he can also think and plan and grapple with more abstract ideas. He does not covet power or position; he is engrossed in his own work, in what he wants to do. He has had several wives, but has reached a touchingly intimate relationship, a marriage of mind as well as body, with his new young wife Metoo. If it had been Mitchison's purpose to do so, she could have written a whole novel about Hands.

Early in Orcadia does not in fact begin with Hands, but with a careful description of an old man sitting on a cliff looking at the sea (pp. 9-10). Given this deliberate introduction one might expect him to be a central character in the episode, but we never learn his name, and he is too old to sail off to the Shining with Hands and Metoo. Yet Mitchison has intentionally placed him in this significant position. He has been a famous hunter in his time and now has an honoured place in the community. He is observant and thoughtful, working at ideas and problems, drawing on the experience of many years. It is he who realises that there are currents in the water which can carry a boat over to the Shining, the discovery on which the whole book depends.

Hands is one of his many sons, and we understand that some at least of the good qualities we see in Hands come from the old man. (Mitchison, with her concern for scientific accuracy, does not fail to point out (p. 19) that, since Hands and his father have both reached a mature age with all their teeth and other faculties intact, there is a good genetic inheritance in this family.) In Mitchison's eyes, in fact, the old man is the ancestor, the originator, in a symbolic as well as real fashion, and that is why he has the place of honour at the beginning of the book.

The characters whom she explores with most empathy and insight, however, are the two women, one at either end of the book, Metoo and Moon Woman. Throughout Mitchison's writing we find women characters who have attained a balance in their lives between mind and body: she gives them intelligence and skill, but also, in full measure, the experience and enjoyment of love, sex, childbirth and motherhood. Metoo can be seen as the centre of the extended family in the new settlement and Hands sees her as 'the wife of his heart' (p. 21). She got her name 'because of how she had been as a girl-child in a big family group: a survivor, that one'. (p. 19) The constant workload of Stone Age woman fills most of her life, but she has the ingenuity (Mitchison imagines) to invent weaving. In old age she becomes 'the one who must always be consulted and listened to' (p. 86), the wise woman of the tribe, a figure to whom Mitchison assigns great importance. In old age – Mitchison lived to be over a hundred years old – she liked, if only half seriously, to think she was such a figure herself.

Moon Woman, when we meet her, is already a wise woman, though at most middle-aged: she is skilled in astronomy, and through this knowledge, like the earlier Big Woman, is a kind of shaman or priestess in her world. She has had a happy marriage and several children. She is young enough at heart, and adventurous enough, to go with the strangers to the unknown place where her skills are needed. Like the professional woman she is, she sets herself to solve the problem presented to her. But there is this intriguing figure, the Sun Man, and in spite of his impressive strength and position, she realises that she has the power to attract him. The last words of the episode, indeed of the book, are in her voice, 'Should I, then?' (p. 176) The reader mentally continues the story – surely she did, and what happened next? – and that can only come about when a character is fully developed, completely alive, a real person, recognisable as not so different from ourselves.

Language
When writing about characters who live so far back in time as Metoo and Hands, Mitchison has to decide what to do about dialogue. We have absolutely no idea how Stone Age people spoke. Mitchison admits that we do not know 'if any words of their language are still in ours'. (p. 5) Nor do we know if what they spoke would be recognisable to us as a language, or if it was as wordless and disjointed as a baby's first attempts at communication. But the baby knows what it wants to say, and so did the Stone Age people. The writer has to get something down on paper which will represent what the characters think and feel.

For instance, concepts like number and measurement are in their infancy, yet Hands and Metoo know there is a difference between one person and more than one person. When someone dies, there is one person less. When another boatful of settlers comes, says Hands, 'we shall be almost many persons.' (p. 83) Similarly, there is a difference between a young child and an old man: the question is only how to express that idea. Mitchison reasonably imagines her characters counting on their fingers, as small children and some primitive tribes do today. 'You count the fingers and thumb. After one count you will have a name ... After two counts you may be given a spear ... At three counts you are a true man.' (p. 11)

But there is more theoretical thinking to be done. Hands, who in today's world would probably be an engineer, is 'someone who looked at things and saw how they could do what he wanted.' (p. 25) Metoo has an inspiration about shearing the sheep: 'Listen. We catch the big ewes. Two hold, one pull, maybe cut.' (p. 61) Mitchison assumes that her characters imagine things, though they can only describe it as 'making pictures in [your] mind.' (p. 68) From that faculty so much is going to develop: storytelling, art, ideas of ghosts and gods.

Besides the question of thinking, there is the question of emotion, and how Hands and Metoo may have expressed what they felt. Naturally we do not know that either, and Mitchison starts by admitting it: 'We can only know that they must have been happy when Spring came, when the sunshine was warm and when they felt the touch of a loved body.' (p. 7)

So this is what Hands and Metoo feel: happiness and comfort, and of course the opposite, anxiety, fear and pain. These are the feelings Mitchison has to make them express, and she does so convincingly. When they snuggle together on a cowskin with their baby, all is 'nice-nice' (p. 26). In a moment of deeper emotion, when Metoo is afraid that Hands will never come back from his visit to the mainland, he reassures her in simple, clumsy, yet perfectly adequate words: 'I cannot not come back. I am you.' (p. 56)

Sometimes Mitchison has to convey a more complicated emotion which her character has no words to express. While Hands is away, the women find a paddle washed up on the shore, which at first they think must be his. 'Metoo yelled with pain.' (p. 77) Of course it is not exactly pain, but shock, fear, grief, which Metoo does not have the vocabulary to describe; but she does have a word for pain. What she feels is strong and unpleasant like pain, so that is the word Mitchison gives her, and it has the required effect for the reader. Even more effective is the rendering of Metoo's state of mind when Hands sails away in the boat Branch. She is sick with worry, but pushes the thought away: 'Branch. Hands. No!' and then she shouts furiously at the others who are left behind (p. 57). She is converting the uncontrollable emotion into one which she can cope with, something everyone has done at times.

As the story goes on from episode to episode, the speakers grow more fluent. Mitchison recognises that once there were meetings between different tribes, there must have been talking. Third-boy finds that the noises made by the stranger, if repeated, seem to mean something, and can be used to communicate (pp. 146-147). By the last episode Moon Woman is even able to cope with a strange accent and understand a slightly different language (p. 165). And Pigsie has got the hang of making those pictures in his head at will, and speaking them out as stories (p. 134). Over the period covered by *Early in Orcadia*, humankind has found its voice.

Myth and religion
If we ask what part belief or religion played in the life of prehistoric man, Mitchison admits 'Nothing tells us of gods or sacrifices ... We can only guess'. (p. 7) Since Stone Age life, as she is depicting it, contained the beginnings of so much that is now apparent in the modern world, she suggests that some form of religion must have existed too, if only in the form of a feeling that there was something beyond the short life of a human being. As with the development of other human abilities and concepts, she traces its possible development over the five episodes of *Early in Orcadia*.

1. Hands and Metoo
Life is short – few people live beyond the age of thirty – and deaths are frequent, especially in the dark winter when food runs short. The bodies of the dead are quickly moved to a roofless, thick-walled house which is not really a house and should not be visited. If anyone does go near, a 'special smoke' has to be made. Obviously, as we see it now, the smoke has disinfectant or fumigating properties, and the whole business of keeping the dead and the living apart is a sensible hygienic precaution. Yet there is some mystery attached to the placing of the bodies in the house. 'Certain things might be done. But it was better not to think about it.' (p. 17)

Sister, the woman who reached the Shining before Hands and Metoo, put her husband and child when they died into such a house, with big stones against the doorway to keep them in (p. 43). Nevertheless she feels the presence of her dead children, 'ghosts now, hungry ghosts. Angry at her.' (p. 37)

Even so early in the story of humankind, Mitchison imagines, there is a feeling that dead people somehow live on. In the commentary following this episode she suggests that people must have wondered whether the bad times of winter and famine could be averted in some way. 'Difficult questions floated up from the dark.' (p. 88) The dead must know about the dark, since they lived there. Might they come back and help the living? How could they be made to do that?

2. Little Honey

By Little Honey's time it is thought that the dead do come back in the bodies of living people: this belief, known as reincarnation, has been held by many societies as a way of explaining how the dead may live on. By now, too, there is a wise woman in the tribe, the Big Woman who is also called the Good Woman. She is thought to be in charge of the moon and to order the growth of crops and the birth of lambs. (In fact, she has acquired some knowledge of what we now call astronomy and agriculture.) (p. 93) Most importantly, she is the intermediary between the tribe and the eagles.

White-tailed sea eagles were once common in Orkney (they later died out, but are being reintroduced in some parts of Scotland). Because of the mysterious discovery that the bones in the tomb at Isbister were intermingled with the bones and claws of eagles, it is thought that they must have been regarded with reverence, as guardians of the tribe or even as gods. Mitchison here shows a possible early stage of such a belief. The Big Woman makes sacrifices to the eagles – human sacrifice, Mitchison implies – and the apprentice potter girl Little Honey must give them her first pot and herself undergo a painful initiation (pp. 106-108). Otherwise the eagles will be angry. No one knows what might happen then, but it is something to be avoided at all costs.

3. Pigsie

Pigsie is helping to build 'the great bone place', a development of the practice of putting the dead, with special ceremonies and rituals, in a house of their own. (It is in fact what we now know as the Tomb of the Eagles at Isbister.) The practice of honouring them continues and the belief in reincarnation is strong. When Pigsie's sister Ba is pregnant she is taken to the bone place and picks out a stone axe-head from among the grave goods, possessions of the dead which have been placed with their bones. From this the keeper of the bones knows (or says he knows) which long-dead member of the tribe will come back to life in the form of her baby (pp. 129-132).

The eagles are also still involved. A mythical Moon Woman who is 'not anywhere ... not a real woman' (p. 117) is now associated with them, as the human Big Woman was at an earlier time, but her functions have been taken over by the keeper of the bones, who is the Sun Man. Mitchison is probably referring to the theory that worship of a pre-Christian mother goddess was at some point overthrown by a newer religion centred on a male god.

4. Third-boy

The old ones of the tribe are now honoured as the Big Woman was in Little Honey's time. In return for their favourite bits of meat they will say 'wise and difficult words' (p. 141) which will help the giver, though he does not know how. When wise old people die 'they do not altogether go. They are not only bones in darkness. We hear them still.' (p. 150) The idea that the dead can help is now linked to these wise old people: they give advice now, and will continue to do so when they are dead.

It is still believed that when people die they go to the eagles, but more thinking has been done about that. Behind the eagles is darkness and 'the Name we do not say' (p. 141). There has always been a feeling that behind the Big Woman and the keeper of the bones, even behind the eagles, there is something much greater. Now, Mitchison suggests, human beings are beginning to imagine this Something, which will eventually become their God.

5. Moon Woman

The keeper of the bones is getting old and is no longer such an important figure in the tribe. Even the bones are less important. There is again a wise woman in the tribe, the Moon Woman. She does not carry out the fearsome sacrifices made by the Big Woman of an earlier time, but like her she is an astronomer, particularly concerned with the movements of the moon (pp. 162-163).

Yet there are elements of religion in her view of the heavenly bodies: the sun and moon, when not visible in the sky, are lighting up 'the Other Place which was full of what had been people' (p. 162), in slightly more modern terms the region of the souls of the dead. A neighbouring tribe is ruled by a Sun Man, who is as much a lord as a priest, just as the Moon Woman is as much an astronomer as a priestess. Similarly, his people honour the sun, who is their 'master and maker'. They have raised a great circle of standing stones 'to show the way of the sun' (p. 169).

Here Mitchison is referring to the theory put forward by Professor Alexander Thom in the 1960s that stone circles and standing stones are in fact astronomical observatories, set up to align with the sun and moon at certain dates, by which prehistoric people could construct a calendar and, among other things, foretell eclipses (this is what the Sun Man asks the Moon Woman to calculate for his tribe). Though some details have been queried, the positioning of many of the circles and stones does seem to bear out the theory in general terms. Mitchison uses it to suggest how prehistoric people might have worked out a satisfactory solution

Early in Orcadia 17

to the problems of gods and the after-life, just as the intelligent and ingenious Hands solved the more practical problems of the Shining. Like speech, art and human fellowship, the concept of religion is seen to develop over the generations spanned by *Early in Orcadia*.

3. The Big House (1950)

The Big House is a children's fantasy novel. For that reason it is not always included in discussions of Naomi Mitchison's fiction, though the poet and critic Alexander Scott, one of its first reviewers, thought very highly of it and described it as a tragi-comedy which weaves together 'the natural magic of childhood, the terrible charm of the supernatural, [and] the dark power of history'.

Considered as a children's book, it is original and full of charm. Mitchison has set it in an area of the West Highlands which she knows well, and which has not often featured in children's fiction (see later, **Setting and language**). The magical and supernatural elements of the story come from the folklore of the area (see later, **Celtic myths and folklore**). The result is a compelling atmosphere of everyday magic, a world which seems to shimmer between reality and myth.

There can, however, be a serious intention in fantasy novels: this has been recognised, for instance, in the Narnia series by C.S. Lewis, and more recently in works by J.K. Rowling (the Harry Potter series) and Philip Pullman (the trilogy *His Dark Materials*). There is certainly a purpose behind *The Big House*. Mitchison has used the form of a children's fantasy to present a problem which greatly concerned her in the Highland community where she lived.

The story of the novel
The first part of *The Big House* (pp. 9-98) begins on Hallowe'en, a night when (as the characters know) ghosts, fairies and other supernatural beings are allowed to mingle with humans. Su, who lives in the Tigh Mòr (the Big House) in the West Highland village of Port-na-Sgadan, is bullied by the village children when she tries to join in the traditional Hallowe'en pastime of guising, going from door to door in fancy dress with false-faces or masks and turnip lanterns. Only Winkie, a fisherman's son, is friendly towards her. Their friendship is an awkward one, and both are aware that this, like the bullying, arises from bad feeling dating from previous generations. 'In times past the Big House ones had been hard and cruel to the fathers and grandfathers of the ones at the school ...' (p. 10)

Su and Winkie hear someone coming along the road playing the bagpipes. The piper, Donald Ferguson, is a stranger looking for help, and they take him into the Big House. He tells Winkie that he is being pursued by 'Yon Ones', the fairies (p. 16). He has been a prisoner in the Fairy Hill for many years and has managed

The Big House

to escape because it is Hallowe'en.

A green-cloaked young man, a prince of the fairy people, arrives (p. 17) to take Donald back to the Hill. Su and Winkie hide him just in time, but the prince spitefully steals Su's shadow (p. 29). It can only be retrieved if Su and Winkie go into the Fairy Hill. They find they have an unexpected helper in their quest: the Brounie (p. 30), the supernatural guardian of Su's family over the centuries, who, unknown to her, has been in the Big House all along.

They are magically transported back in time to the early nineteenth century (p. 36), to find that Su is still a child of the Big House but Winkie is a downtrodden tenant's son. They are kept apart by their social position – at that time, rich and poor children would never meet – but, with the Brounie's help, manage to get together (pp. 45-46) and find the entrance to the Fairy Hill. The world inside the hill is all they could have wished for, but the beauty is only an illusion and vanishes when they refuse the fairy prince's gift (p. 72). The king of the fairies tries to tempt them to stay, but Su recovers her shadow and they return to the present day (p. 79).

But the fairy prince appears again, still in pursuit of his prisoner. To keep the piper in this world, Su has to endure the ordeal of holding on to him while he goes through a series of magical transformations. He turns into a snake, a slater (or woodlouse), a wild deer, a bar of white-hot iron, but she holds tight, and he is finally changed into a small baby (pp. 89-90). In that form he can stay in the present day and will be brought up in the Big House.

The second part of the novel (pp. 99-169) begins when Su comes home after her first term at boarding-school in England. She and Winkie have lost touch and he hangs around with his friends from the village, while she spends her time with her brothers and friends from school. Then magic intervenes again: the fairies steal baby Donald's soul, and now he is a changeling, an unpleasant fairy child (p. 104).

The Brounie appears and explains that the fairies have done this to revenge themselves on Su. She will have to go back in time to rescue Donald's soul. The magic used for the last journey cannot work without Winkie, and to go on her own Su will have to take another route, in some other form (pp. 107-109). She chooses to turn into a swan.

The swan Su circles over Port-na-Sgadan, going farther back in time with each circuit she makes (pp. 110-113). When she finally lands at some point during the Dark Ages, she is shot at by a young man, who is Winkie. As the arrow strikes her wing she changes back to human form. She is carried to the castle, which stands on the site where the Big House will later be. She is regarded as a magical swan-maiden and treated with respect, even by the family priest, who has carefully put away the swan feathers by which she was able to fly.

Winkie has come into the past to find her, with the Brounie's help (pp. 121-124), and in this time he is a chieftain. His father has been killed, and to avenge him he in turn is about to kill the captured killer, but Su begs for the prisoner's life (p. 133). It was a fairy woman who told Winkie to shoot a lone swan when it appeared (p. 126); she knew it would be Su. She will come back in seven days to see if he has obeyed.

When she appears, her magic almost persuades Winkie to trust her instead of Su, but she is overpowered by holy water sprinkled by Su and the priest, and reveals what has happened to Donald's soul (pp. 141-145). It is in the shape of a golden hazelnut, hidden 'under the stone of the boar'. Winkie is summoned to a council at the hill of Dun Add, where there is an ancient crowning stone carved with a boar. They find the golden hazelnut and Su is ready to go home (pp. 156-157).

But Winkie likes being a chieftain and wants to stay in the past. Su learns that the priest has burned her swan feathers and so she cannot go back as she came. It seems she is stranded in the past, but the Brounie comes to the rescue. Even then there is no easy way to get home. They will have to go together. It is a great wrench for Winkie to give up his life as a chieftain, but he agrees for Su's sake. They hold hands and are transported back to the present day (pp. 158-160). They are still at Dun Add, miles from Port-na-Sgadan, but they are given a lift in a lorry; magically, the driver is Winkie's prisoner who in the past was saved by Su (pp. 163-166). Back at the Big House, they complete their quest by returning baby Donald's soul.

No longer a swan maiden and a chieftain, they are the children Su and Winkie once more; but the Brounie has promised Winkie that he will have a chieftain's power again when he is a man. And Su finds that the birthmark she has always had on her arm is exactly where the arrow struck her wing when she was a swan (p. 169). Everyday life in Port-na-Sgadan and their magic adventures touch and overlap.

Theme and structure of the novel
The theme of *The Big House* is class division, the distrust and even dislike which may be felt between people in different social positions. It is expressed through the story of two children of

The Big House

different backgrounds, Su from the Big House and Winkie from the village.

Naomi Mitchison had a lifelong dream of a world in which all men and women should be equal, where friendship and love should not be governed by ideas of social class. When she moved to live in the Big House of the West Highland village of Carradale in the late 1930s, she hoped that she, though the laird, would be able to form friendships with the villagers. She found it difficult to become fully accepted. This is the problem she works out in *The Big House*. She uses magic and time-travel to show Su and Winkie, the next generation, how artificial and unnecessary any division between them must be.

The structure of the novel is intended to make this clear. At a first reading it may seem awkward, since the action of the story falls into two distinct parts – Su and Winkie have two virtually separate adventures, in different periods of time – but Mitchison has planned this with care.

'It would be a queer world,' says Winkie at one point, 'if the same ones were aye up or aye down. It isna that way that things go.' (p. 123) When we first see Su and Winkie in the middle of the twentieth century, they are more or less on the same level. They know each other and go to the same school, and there is really nothing to stop them being friends. But in the early nineteenth century, as we see in the first time-travel episode, Su's family in the Big House is much farther 'up' in terms of social position, with much more power than in the present day, while Winkie's family is 'down', half-starved ragged tenants despised and ill-treated by the Big House. We now understand how, in present-day Port-na-Sgadan, old memories and resentment have come down through their families to the village children, making them act out a hostility which belongs to past generations.

We have also learned, almost in passing, that Su and Winkie in fact belong to the same family. 'Yon laddie is far oot kin o' yours on the mither's side,' says the Brounie. 'In this time [the nineteenth century] his name is the same as your ain.' (p. 49) It is only that one branch of the family is 'up' and the other 'down', and Mitchison wants to make it clear that these are temporary and unimportant positions. That is why we have the second time-travel adventure, when Su goes back to the Dark Ages. There she finds Winkie, and in that time he is the one who is 'up', a chieftain living in a castle, with the power of life and death over his enemies.

We have been shown that the social class of a family can change. To underline the message, Mitchison links the different episodes by means of the tinker girl Dina, who appears several times (pp. 20-21, 87-94, 102-104, 113-116, 152-153). Tinkers or travellers, who are still to be found in many parts of Scotland and were regular visitors to the Carradale area when Mitchison was writing *The Big House*, are a living example of a social group whose status has changed. Nowadays they are all too often treated as vagabonds and outcasts, for no reason except the distrust which people may feel for anybody with a different lifestyle. But *tinker* was originally only a name for the craft of metalworker. In the Dark Ages episode of *The Big House* the tinkers are seen at their trade, making 'all of our swords and spearheads ... and cooking pots and pans forby that' (p. 146), an essential and honoured part of the community. Mitchison draws on tradition to suggest further that the tinkers are in touch with the magical powers which also appear throughout the novel, uniting its different parts.

Characters
The main characters in *The Big House* are Su and Winkie, whose quests, first for Su's shadow and to save the piper, and then for baby Donald's soul, form the story. In the plan of the book they are not just two children, but representatives of their respective social classes. The difficulty for a writer is that if this intention is too obvious, the book becomes a manifesto or a sermon, not a novel. In Mitchison's hands Su and Winkie remain real children throughout, not always right, occasionally not even likeable, and the more believable because of that.

Su, aged ten, lives in the Big House with only the old servant Morag for company. She goes to the village school but has not been able to make friends, except, tentatively, with Winkie, and she is lonely, with 'the awful feeling of being different'. This is largely due to the village's old resentment of the Big House, but we can also see that Su has a slightly bossy manner at times, and that she and the other children have few interests in common. She has moments of bursting into tears (and doting on baby Donald, which Winkie finds somewhat boring), but she proves herself a brave and tough person in the time-travel adventures and the encounters with magic powers.

Winkie's real name is Willie Macrae and he is a fisherman's son who means to go to the fishing himself when he leaves school. (A winkie, from which he gets his nickname, is a guiding light used in ring-net fishing.) Where Su is bossy he is shy, but he can be determined, even obstinate, when he believes he is right. He can be thoughtless and occasionally cruel, but Mitchison shows us how, with his good and bad qualities in balance, he has the potential for leadership.

The Brounie tells Su and Winkie what has happened, after they themselves returned to the present day, to the people whose bodies they inhabited in the time-travel episodes. The nineteenth-century Susan, expected by her family to lead a comfortable upper-class life, became a social reformer and died of a fever caught in the slums (pp. 79-80). The Dark Ages Winkie, on course to be a fighter and ruler, became a saint instead (pp. 165-166). Mitchison wants us to understand that nobody's future is fixed, no one is to be pigeonholed in a career or way of life because of social class; neither these people of the past, nor the present-day Su and Winkie, nor anyone else.

Setting and language
The village of Port-na-Sgadan in *The Big House* can be recognised as the village of Carradale in Kintyre, south Argyll, where Mitchison lived for most of her long life. (Port-na-Sgadan means 'port of the herring', a suitable name for a fishing village, but it is also the name of a township near Carradale.) The Tigh Mòr or Big House where Su lives is Carradale House, Mitchison's home. In a diary published as *Among You Taking Notes* (1985) Mitchison describes how she went guising through the village, as both children and adults do in *The Big House*.

Dun Add, now usually spelled Dunadd, is a rocky outcrop in Mid Argyll, prominent in the middle of the flat marshland known as the Moine Mhòr or Great Moss of Crinan. It became the site of a fort at least fifteen hundred years ago. The stone with a carving of a boar found by Su and Winkie can still be seen.

In writing this novel, so closely linked to Carradale and to her own relationship with Carradale people, Mitchison has used a 'Carradale voice'. On coming to live in the West Highlands she was greatly attracted by the soft accents she heard around her. Gaelic, once the language of the area, was no longer much used in everyday life, but Carradale speech in English contained Gaelic words and Gaelic-influenced phrases, and this is the speech of most of the characters in *The Big House*. 'He has stolen your shadow on you,' says the piper (p. 29), and the fairy prince says in his coolly threatening way, 'Is it back with me you are coming, Donal Beg?' (p. 88)

Mitchison uses this Carradale speech not only in dialogue but in the narrative of the novel. This is particularly noticeable in the first chapter when she is setting the scene and atmosphere of the story: 'It is this way it always is on Hallowe'en' (p. 11); also in the last chapter, where in a similar way Su and Winkie are poised between reality and magic: 'It was kind of nasty, the sound of yon hard whistle in the middle of the blackness, and for a moment there was a scare on both the two children' (p. 163). Added to her use of local West Highland folklore, this has the effect of unifying place, people and story.

Su is not a native of the village and generally speaks standard English, often using slang phrases which may seem slightly dated to us now: 'What rot, what utter rot, Winkie!' (p. 16) She has picked up some local phrases: 'He's away better than a fisherman, anyway!' (p. 28)

Midway through the book, when she comes home with an English school friend, and her brothers are also home from their boarding-school, the narrative is in standard English: this is the language in Su's mind. 'Su came back from her first term at an English school aching to be home, and yet feeling it strange. ... Polly wasn't half bad ... Hugh was batty about fishing now.' (p. 99) When she speaks to the village boys, her thoughts are phrased in local speech again: 'But she had a sore feel on her, and soon enough she was back with her own lot.' (p. 101) Winkie's thoughts, immediately afterwards, are presented in Carradale speech: 'Although it was aye jagging him to write, he never got round to it' (p. 101), and he has noticed 'her big brothers with their fine high-class voices that they had now.' (pp. 101-102) Mitchison is using these speech patterns to point out once more the awkward gap between the village and the Big House, which now, for the first time in the present-day story of the novel, contains a 'high-class' household, not just Su.

Historical periods
a) 1945-6

The present day of the novel, to which Su and Winkie return with mingled relief and regret after their time-travelling, is located precisely by Mitchison in the years 1945-6, just after the end of World War II. The living conditions of that time would have been familiar enough to the first readers of *The Big House*. When the novel was published in 1950, for instance, food rationing was still in force, and nobody in Scotland yet had television. Now, more than fifty years later, some explanation may be required.

The opening sentence of the novel sets the scene: 'This was Hallowe'en, and the end of the black-out which had spoiled everything all these years' (p. 9). Su remembers once or twice how all windows had to be heavily curtained, and Hallowe'en guising, parading through the streets with turnip lanterns, has been impossible. For fear of air-raids, virtually no lights could be shown out of doors during the war. Even Winkie's torch, which comes in useful when their time-travelling lands them on Dun Add at midnight (p. 161), would have had to be shielded so that only a glimmer escaped.

Welcoming the piper to the Big House, Su can only offer him bread and margarine 'because, as usual, the butter ration was finished' (p. 26). Food was strictly rationed during the war and for some years afterwards. The rationing included sweets, which is why the fairy prince tempts Su and Winkie with 'pre-war chocolates' (p. 18). When Donald Ferguson returns to the present as a baby, he may have escaped from the Fairy Hill but he still needs a ration book, which fortunately is no problem for the Brounie (p. 91). (He also needs an identity card, carried by all, even babies, for security reasons.) Su acts as hostess because her mother is in London on war work (p. 24). As her father plays no part in the story, Mitchison does not mention him, and there is no need to explain his absence; readers would assume he is in the forces, like so many fathers during the war.

Su and Winkie have probably never heard of television. The newly-launched BBC television service had closed down in 1939, and would not reach Scotland for another six or seven years. The Big House gets its electricity from an 'engine', a generator (p. 15), and the electric lights fascinate Winkie because he does not have them at home; there is no mains electricity yet in Port-na-Sgadan, and most houses would use oil-lamps. We may even notice with some surprise the clothes which the Brounie supplies for baby Donald (p. 91). A dress? A petticoat? Two shawls? And all in delicate natural fabrics, definitely not machine-washable. But then nobody had a washing machine.

But in this strange transitional period which now seems almost as far away as the Dark Ages, there was an atmosphere of optimism which Mitchison must have seen as fitting the theme of her book. The war had been won. The servicemen and women were coming home. A Labour Government had been elected in Britain. Su and Winkie live in a post-war world, and things are going to change. It is a good time to question the old rules and conventions of social class.

b) 1805

We can work out accurately the date when Su first finds herself in the past. She has gone back 'twice seventy years' to the time when the piper was abducted into the Fairy Hill (pp. 24, 32), and so it is

1805. The Big House is the same house, but full of people, 'made alive and lit up with voices and candles, music and mealtimes' (p. 37), unlike the lonely house of 1945. Mitchison has given us a good picture of the post-war world, and now we have a detailed view of Scottish upper-class domestic life in the early nineteenth century. Su, with her twentieth-century consciousness, notices a few less desirable things about 1805 life: no water supply, for instance, and the servants having to empty the chamber-pots (p. 41).

Her observation of the servants – 'They don't seem to mind. *Why* don't they mind?' – is very relevant to Mitchison's purpose. Su hears, even if she does not fully understand, the grown-ups' talk about 'the common people getting uppish and speaking against their betters ... getting together to ask for more wages, against all law and decency' (p. 43). There is unrest elsewhere, and here in Port-na-Sgadan the tailor is spreading the gospel of a radical organisation called the United Scotsmen. Winkie explains to Su, 'They are the ones that will get us freedom – and votes – and no' to be put out of our houses when the laird says' (p. 50). It is useful for us to be aware, though Su and Winkie cannot know in 1805, that the next quarter-century will be one of working-class protest, strikes and mass arrests, and that there will be moves towards parliamentary reform, with a Reform Act in 1832. Just as in 1945, Scottish society in 1805 is at a point of change. That is why Mitchison has chosen to bring her characters back twice seventy years.

c) **The Dark Ages**
In contrast to Mitchison's precision in the other periods, the dating of the second time-travel episode is somewhat vague. Again we have a vivid picture of domestic life in the past, but when Su tries to find out exactly when in the past, the best she can discover is that 'there was a King in Edinburgh, and there was a Lord of the Isles'. She thinks it must be somewhere in the time known as the Dark Ages, 'before you got to William Wallace or Mary Queen of Scots or anyone you could be really interested in' (p. 115). As she muses later, 'They aren't so fussy about time as we are ... and maybe it's better that way' (p. 138). If we want to be fussy, we can probably date this episode around AD 1000, give or take a couple of hundred years.

In this indefinite period Winkie is a Chief, ruling over his people but himself subject to the Lord of the Isles. What we are seeing is an early form of the clan system which prevailed in the Highlands until the eighteenth century; it was banned after the

The Big House

battle of Culloden in 1746, and other elements of social change were also making it less viable at that time. (As we have seen, by 1805 the relationship between chief and people was very different.) Mitchison thought it a good arrangement and would have liked her lairdship at Carradale to follow similar lines. In her depiction of the Dark Ages, the system works well.

She provides a glimpse of a still earlier model of society, centred on the rock of Dun Add where, it is thought, the kings of Dalriada (corresponding roughly to modern Argyll) were crowned. More accurately, they were confirmed in their position by the vote of all their people, in Mitchison's view an ideal co-operation. She further suggests that this co-operation in the choice of ruler extends to supernatural powers: Winkie says 'The stone of the Boar [on Dun Add] is the old stone of crowning, and there could be spirits there that would not maybe like to be woken at night.' (p. 155) As in her depiction of the tinkers, Mitchison is implying that the magical elements in the life of Port-na-Sgadan have always been there, more acknowledged in earlier times than in the mid-twentieth century which is home to Su and Winkie.

Celtic myths and folklore

The supernatural beings in *The Big House* are from the folklore of the West Highlands. The fairies who play such an important part in the story are not little fluttering creatures who live in flowers, but Celtic fairies, and in this tradition the fairy people are tall and handsome, descendants of the gods, living in palaces beneath the ground. More often than not they are malevolent; it is dangerous even to refer to them by name, and Winkie calls them 'Yon Ones' (p. 16). Certainly they are not to be trusted. Their most noticeable quality, apart from their beauty, is a coldness: they have no kind feelings, no pity, no conscience. These are the opponents whom Su and Winkie have to face.

Some of the other figures and concepts from Celtic folklore which Mitchison uses in *The Big House* are listed below.

The **Brounie**, or brownie, is a friendly being who lives in a particular house and looks after the family. He is generally helpful (hence the use of the name for junior Girl Guides with their promise to 'help other people at all times'). He keeps an eye on the servants and himself carries out household tasks during the night, though he is offended if offered any payment or reward. In Kintyre, where there are several well-known brownie traditions, the name is always pronounced brounie or broonie; that is why Mitchison uses this spelling for Su and Winkie's Brounie.

A **changeling** is a fairy left in the cradle in place of a human baby, who is taken by the fairies to be brought up as their own. The changeling is a wizened little old creature, skinny and ugly, who cries constantly and never grows or thrives however well it is fed. The recommended solution, which the Brounie mentions to Su (p. 107), was to pretend to be going to throw the changeling on the fire; alternatively it could be left by the seashore to be drowned. The fairies would swoop down and rescue it in the nick of time, restoring the human baby.

Fairy hills, small green mounds which are the homes of fairies, occur in both Irish and Scottish folklore, and such hillocks are found all over the Highlands, generally called Knocknashee or some similar name (*cnoc na sidhe*, hill of the fairies). Damaging them or digging into them brings bad luck. Where they have been excavated by unsuperstitious archaeologists, they often prove to be prehistoric burial mounds. Music is often heard from fairy hills, and the story of the piper in *The Big House* (pp. 26-27) is a common one: a particularly skilful musician is lured into the hill to play at a fairy wedding, only emerging many years later, if at all. Other humans are abducted because the fairy queen finds them attractive: Su's ordeal in holding on to the piper through magical transformations comes directly from the Scottish border ballad *Tam Lin*, which has that kind of story line. The world inside the hill is full of beauty and luxury, though often, as in *The Big House*, this is found to be all an illusion. Above all, humans in the fairy hill must not eat, drink or accept gifts, or they will never be able to leave. Fortunately, Su and Winkie know this rule (pp. 68, 70, 72).

Hallowe'en, 31st October, was the last day of the Celtic year and a significant date. It was the eve of Samhain, one of the four Celtic quarter days, the others being the first days of February, May and August. Being on the boundary between seasons – in the case of Hallowe'en, between years – these days were also between worlds, and the barriers between reality and the supernatural world dissolved. On Hallowe'en the spirits of the dead could visit the world of the living, the origin of some of the spooky symbols used in Hallowe'en celebrations today. On Hallowe'en, too, human beings could enter a fairy hill, and – most important in *The Big House* – only on Hallowe'en could a human prisoner in the fairy hill hope to escape.

Swan maidens, young women who sometimes become swans (or vice versa), are found in folk tales all over the world. Generally a man steals a swan maiden's feathers, or swan dress, which she has laid aside to bathe. She has to remain in human form until she finds the feathers, and then flies away. In *The Big House* the story has a twist, since the priest burns Su's feathers and she cannot turn back into a swan (pp. 157-158). Mitchison uses the swan maiden legend, again with developments of her own, in what is probably her best short story, 'Five Men and a Swan'.

4. Travel Light (1952)

Travel Light, as its title suggests, is the story of a journey, but this is a journey with magical elements. The heroine Halla travels not only through different countries but through time. The setting shifts too between reality and fantasy. Halla is brought up first among bears and then among dragons, but her journey later takes her to the Micklegard, the real city called Byzantium or Constantinople in historical times, now Istanbul.

It is also a journey through Halla's life. She is not always sure who she is or where she is heading. The qualities and abilities she develops along the way help her to deal with later problems; that happens in everybody's life, even if not everybody is fireproofed by dragons or able to talk to animals. Like everybody, too, she has choices to make on the journey, though perhaps the fates are weaving the pattern of her destiny, unseen.

Why does Naomi Mitchison mingle fantasy and reality, myth and history, in *Travel Light*? She is suggesting that magic – or an awareness that there may be more to life that meets the eye – is needed in the modern world (and Micklegard/Byzantium is 'modern' in its culture of political corruption and bribery). Halla, in touch with the forces of nature and the world of myth, is needed in the mean streets of Micklegard.

The story of the novel

Halla is the daughter of a king. Her mother dies soon after she is born and her stepmother tells the king to get rid of the baby. Her nurse Matulli saves her by taking the shape of a bear and carrying her off into the forest (p. 11).

Halla is brought up with the bear-cubs and learns to talk to animals. But she is still a human being, and Matulli worries that their lifestyles will soon become incompatible (pp. 11-13). A dragon, Uggi, appears and Matulli tells him the story of Halla Bearsbairn. Since she has been badly treated by a king and queen, and kings are among the enemies of dragons, he offers to adopt her and Halla rides off on his back (pp. 14-16).

The dragons welcome her as part of Uggi's treasure. She is fireproofed at once (p. 17) to avoid accidents (since dragons breathe fire), and lives happily with the dragons, learning about their irresistible desire for gold and their feud with men. It is a great shock when Uggi tells her that she is not a dragon (p. 24). A Valkyrie, Steinvor, arriving on a winged horse, tells Halla that she is out of place on Dragon Mountain and invites her to join

Travel Light

the Valkyries on their mission to carry fallen heroes to Valhalla (pp. 30-32). (See later, **Norse myths and legends**.) Halla prefers to stay with the dragons, but she is unsettled. Steinvor has suggested that the Norns – the Fates – may have a different plan for her.

The dragons' habit of seizing animals and treasure from human settlements begins to antagonise the men of the district, whose weaponry has greatly improved in recent years (pp. 35-36). A young dragon is killed (p. 36), and an expedition to avenge him and win more treasure ends in disaster for the dragons. Uggi is killed by a king's son, who invades Dragon Mountain to plunder the dragons' treasure cave. Halla is captured, but rescued by another dragon (pp. 41-43).

She feels neither entirely dragonish nor bearish now (pp. 45-46), and wonders if the Norns do indeed have a different fate planned for her. With some satisfaction she sees her enemy the king's son being killed in a skirmish and collected by Steinvor (p. 48). Halla takes his collar, rings and bracelets, some of Uggi's treasure, meaning to hoard it as a dragon would. But it weighs her down so that she cannot move easily, and she begins to suspect all the creatures in the forest of wanting her gold (pp. 49-51).

In this unhappy state she meets the Wanderer, whom she recognises as Odin, All-Father, chief of the Norse gods (p. 55). She realises that her dragonish love of gold is holding her back, and gives up the treasure. The Wanderer summons a unicorn for her, gives her a piece of his cloak, and sets her on her way, telling her to 'travel light' (p. 57).

She makes a long, dreamlike journey, first riding the unicorn and then by boat down a great river. She talks to animals and birds and finds that she can also speak all human languages. The Wanderer's cloak makes people trust her and treat her well. She drifts down the River Dnieper to Kiev – she is in a real place and time now – and embarks on a ship bound for Micklegard, the fabulous city where she has heard that a Great Dragon lives (pp. 57-60).

Three men come aboard; one of them, Tarkan Der, is descended from the Corn Kings of Marob and their form of Christianity still has some relationship to that pagan religion. They are on their way to Micklegard to complain about the tyrant who governs their country of Marob, certain that the Emperor – the Great Dragon – will help them because he is the representative of God. They ask Halla to come with them and act as their interpreter. They think she must have been sent by God to help them, and call her Halla Godsgift (pp. 62-63).

In Micklegard they find that the original simple form of Christianity has become corrupted by political ambition. There are factions and feuds at court and bribery will be needed to reach the Emperor (pp. 66-71). Halla talks to the horses at the racing stables and gets information about the results of forthcoming chariot races, which are usually fixed. She tells the Marob men how to bet, and with their winnings they are able to bribe the Emperor's servants, though Halla begins to be suspected as a witch (pp. 74-83).

The Marob men see the Emperor and he agrees to dismiss the tyrannous governor (pp. 97-101). They are allowed to return to Marob, but Halla's powers of forecasting are valuable to the courtiers and she is to stay. Steinvor the Valkyrie snatches her up and drops her on board the ship bound for Marob (p. 114).

Two of the men land at Marob, but Tarkan Der's girlfriend has been killed by the tyrant in his absence and he does not want to go home (pp. 118-121). He and Halla travel north, making for the city of Holmgard (now Novgorod). He is becoming fond of Halla, though a little wary of her powers, and proposes to marry her, but she is uneasy. She does not think this is part of All-Father's plan (pp. 122-128).

They reach a settlement not far from Novgorod and hear good reports of Modolf, the head man. During the night the settlement is attacked by enemies and the house is torched with Modolf inside. Halla, long ago fireproofed by dragons, goes into the flames and rescues him (pp. 129-132).

Tarkan becomes interested in Modolf's daughter, to Halla's relief. Modolf's family has had bad luck for generations, ever since, long ago and far up north, a baby princess was cast out to die. Halla realises that she is that princess, and assures Modolf that his bad luck is over (pp. 138-139).

Tarkan will marry Modolf's daughter and take service with the Prince of Holmgard, but Halla knows that her travels are not finished. Steinvor and the Valkyries come back, and this time Halla goes with them. She drops All-Father's cloak behind her, no longer needed. She can travel light (pp. 142-147).

The structure of the novel
Travel Light is divided into three parts of almost equal length (part II, the Micklegard section, is slightly the longest). Mitchison sees the action of the novel in three phases.

Part I (pp. 11-51): Halla is growing up with bears and dragons. She assumes that she is a dragon and acquires dragonish accomplishments. About the half-way point of the section, some doubt creeps into her mind. By the last chapter of part I she realises that she is neither a bear nor a dragon: that phase of her life is at an end.

Part II (pp. 55-102) begins when Halla meets the Wanderer. This is a turning-point in the novel: later (p. 65) she says 'Afterwards all was changed'. She begins the long journey to Micklegard, at first not knowing why. The arrival of the men from Marob brings her role into focus, and their quest to get justice from the Emperor provides the driving force for the section. This phase ends when they have seen the Emperor and their mission is over.

Part III (pp. 105-147): we – like Halla – are in search of a resolution, an answer to the question she finally voices: 'What kind of game has All-Father been having with me?' (p. 145). She travels north with Tarkan Der but they are not really on the same wavelength. Halla's future is not to be in Micklegard, nor in Marob, nor in marriage with Tarkan Der, nor in Modolf's settlement. 'I am still myself,' she thinks (p. 143). Mitchison provides no actual answer to her question. Halla realises that there is no answer, and that none is needed. She finds at last that she is able to stop questioning and accept whatever happens, and this is the meaning of All-Father's instruction to travel light.

Characters

Halla, the girl brought up by bears and dragons, is the only character in *Travel Light* whom Mitchison has fully developed. The other humans – Tarkan Der and his companions, and the rulers and courtiers in Micklegard – are seen mainly through her eyes. Tarkan Der comes to life briefly in his concern for his girl Sweetfeather back in Marob and his grief when he hears she has been killed (p. 101). Essentially, however, he is an ordinary young man who rather likes, but respects and is wary of, the somewhat extraordinary Halla.

The bears are bearish and the dragons are dragonish, and this is all Mitchison requires of them. They are there to illustrate the comfortable but limited world of bears and the treasure-obsessed world of dragons, neither of which is the proper place for Halla.

Halla is an individual, a person searching for herself. Her life moves through several phases, which Mitchison marks by the successive nicknames she receives. (This is a Norse custom: Viking chieftains, for instance, might be known as Erik the Red or Magnus Barelegs.) First she is Halla Bearsbairn (p. 14), but as she quickly outgrows the bear lifestyle, this can be only a temporary phase. Then she is Halla Heroesbane (p. 26), more in prediction than in celebration (she never does kill any heroes, though it is true they are not her favourite people). After the catastrophic attack on Dragon Mountain she thinks of herself as Halla Dragonweeper (p. 45). The men from Marob call her Halla Godsgift (p. 64) in recognition of her otherworldly abilities, and, apart from a brief suggestion of Halla Pathfinder (p. 123), this is the name which stays with her.

Each name fixes a particular characteristic in our minds: it is an apt way to present a fully-developed character, three-dimensional as a real person would be. Mitchison implies that as Halla acquires these names and thinks about what they mean, she is forming a picture of herself in her own mind too. But in spite of the different names there is a basic Halla, a person of a straightforward simplicity whom Mitchison particularly sets in contrast to the plotters of Micklegard. She comes out of a mythical world into reality. If we see all the other characters through her eyes, that is because she is the centre round which the whole story turns. Unchanged herself, she intrigues, mystifies or even changes everyone she meets.

Setting in time and place
It is impossible to say that *Travel Light* is set in any specific place or time. The background to Halla's adventures is sometimes a real city or area, but sometimes belongs to the world of fairy-tales and legends, and at one point she visits a fictional country created by Mitchison in a previous novel. Halla moves from fantasy to reality without noticing any difference, and probably the best way to read the novel is to take these transitions for granted as she does; in this way we too travel light. However, it will help us to appreciate Mitchison's skill if we note some of the backgrounds and settings used, and how smoothly the story moves from one to another.

We begin in the world of fairy-tale. The king's jealous second wife who wants to get rid of the baby princess is a familiar figure from stories like *Snow White*, and this is the situation at the opening of *Travel Light* (p. 11). The baby is saved by her faithful nurse Matulli, and Mitchison neatly moves into another gear by bringing in the motif of shape-shifting, frequently found in folk tales (see later, **Norse myths and legends**).

Finmark or Finnmark, Matulli's home, is a real district in the north of Norway, and Halla's time with the bears is spent in a Scandinavian forest, with its cranberry bushes and its wolves, reindeer and elk (pp. 12-14). Mitchison is drawing here on the many legends of children brought up with animals, like Mowgli with the wolves in *The Jungle Book*. Some of these animal-fostering stories may be based on fact, but Mitchison takes a purposeful step away from reality again with the introduction of the dragon Uggi (p. 14).

Dragons are imaginary creatures, and so Halla's time with them is spent in a mythical world inhabited by other figures from myth and legend. The arrival of Steinvor the Valkyrie (p. 30) confirms that it is specifically the world of Norse mythology, and the Wanderer whom Halla meets (p. 55) is Odin, chief of the Norse gods.

Halla sets off on a long journey, vividly seen yet mysterious, like a journey in a dream. She leaves the mythical country of the dragons, riding on a unicorn, passing 'endless trees and cliffs under the swinging moon', swimming across 'a great waste of waters'. She is 'endlessly far from the lands she had lived in', outside of space and time. But then she transfers to a boat and drifts down 'a wide, slow river', passing ordinary human settlements inhabited by farmers and fishermen. She is travelling 'down the Dnieper to Kiev' (pp. 57-60).

Something very strange has happened, as we realise even if Halla does not: at some point on the journey she has come out of the mythical world and into historical time. Kiev is a real city, founded in the fifth century AD, now the capital of Ukraine. Halla is travelling to Micklegard, the name used by the Norse adventurers known as Vikings for the city which is now Istanbul. Originally the Greek city-state of Byzantium, it was renamed Constantinople in AD 330 when the Emperor Constantine the Great moved his capital there from Rome. The Byzantine Empire took over from the glories of the Roman Empire, and the city became, as Mitchison shows us, a magnet for travellers and adventurers, a rich and powerful city strategically placed between Europe and Asia.

We can even make a rough guess at the date of Halla's visit, because Mitchison mentions 'the Emperor's Guards, the Varangians' (p. 113). The Varangian Guard, composed of men from Sweden, was formed in AD 980. There is no sign that the city has yet been conquered by the Crusaders, which happened in the early thirteenth century, so Halla has probably reached Micklegard somewhere in the eleventh or twelfth century AD.

We can follow Halla's journey on a map from Kiev down to Micklegard, and later from Micklegard all the way up to Holmgard in the north; this was the Viking name for Novgorod, founded in the ninth century AD as a trading city on the river Volkhov. But we are off the map when her ship puts in at 'a certain place called Marob' (p. 62), because Marob is a fictional country, the setting of Mitchison's epic novel *The Corn King and the Spring Queen* (1931). That novel is set in the first and second centuries BC, when the religion of Marob was based on fertility rituals intended to bring about a good harvest. A thousand years later, in *Travel Light*, Marob is Christian, but Tarkan Der is descended from the Corn Kings (p. 65). Probably we are to understand that he is a descendant of the Spring Queen in the earlier novel, Erif Der. Mitchison uses the idea of Marob, with its simple version of Christianity influenced by older beliefs, to criticise the heavily politicised religion now found in Micklegard.

When, towards the end of *Travel Light*, Halla reaches a Norse settlement near Holmgard (p. 129), we discover that Mitchison has played tricks with time as well as location. Halla's abandonment as a baby, which we have assumed was modelled on a fairy-tale, really happened, but it happened many centuries ago, far outwith anybody's life-span. Halla's journey has taken her through time as well as geographical space. She tries to find out from Steinvor the Valkyrie how much time has passed since they first met: 'Five years? Five hundred years?' (p. 145). There is no answer, and finally it does not matter, because Halla, going with the Valkyries on her winged horse, is lifting off out of this world and out of time.

Themes

The two themes which can be picked out in *Travel Light* recur throughout Mitchison's work. First is the importance of the individual human being in a world where priority is all too often given to political and commercial demands. Halla preserves her essential self against the desire for treasure implanted by her upbringing with dragons, and against the power games of Micklegard. It is easy to transpose her situations to the present day and imagine a modern hero confronted by morally dubious practices in big business or politics.

In addition, Halla maintains her position as an independent-minded woman against the forces of conventionality, a position which Mitchison herself often had to defend. Halla is different. She lives with bears but is not a bear, with dragons but is not a dragon. She does not care for heroes, first because they are the enemies of dragons (p. 14), and then because she is captured and nearly raped by one (p. 43). Marriage with Tarkan Der does not appeal to her. (It is partly out of respect for the conventions that he proposes – it is 'not right' (p. 128) for them to travel together unmarried – and he is worried by her magic powers, which make her even more different.) She turns down the opportunity to join the Valkyries (pp. 31-32), but at last accepts (p. 146) because, by her own decision, it is now the right thing for her to do.

The second theme in *Travel Light* is the importance of magic. In much of Mitchison's fiction, even where the setting and narrative are realistic, there is an element of the supernatural, though the characters may be uneasy (like Tarkan Der) about what appears to be happening.

Magic in Mitchison's work has strong links with pagan beliefs about the earth. Fertility, growth, the procession of the seasons were mysterious processes to early humans, and so myths grew up to provide an explanation, and rituals were developed in an attempt to control or influence these events, which were literally matters of life and death. Magic in Mitchison's view, therefore, belongs to the dawn of humankind in a simpler and more innocent world.

She is suggesting that the modern world ought not to lose touch with these early beliefs. Because *Travel Light* is a fantasy, Halla has actual magic powers, such as the ability to talk to animals: for instance, she talks and listens to the hounds, hawks and horses on the ship sailing to Micklegard (p. 61), and, usefully, the racehorses of the Hippodrome (pp. 74-76). If, again, we transpose her situation to the present day, we can see how a sensitivity to all life and an openness to beliefs and experience – qualities which Mitchison herself possessed – are being proposed as a counterbalance to the complications and corruptions of a materialistic world.

Norse myths and legends
Halla's early life takes place against a background of Norse folklore. Many of the visitors to Dragon Mountain, such as trolls, giants and the Boygg (pp. 28-29), are figures from Scandinavian folk tales. (Unicorns and mermaids occur more often in other traditions.) The ancestors lamented by the Grendel family (p. 26) meet their fate in the Old English epic poem *Beowulf*, which is set in Scandinavia.

Dragons themselves, though found in folklore and legends all over the world (think of the splendid dragons in Chinese art), have a considerable presence in Scandinavian stories, with their fiery breath and their treasure-hoards. The climax of *Beowulf* is a fight in which the hero and the dragon are both killed, and Beowulf is buried with the dragon's treasure heaped around him.

Shape-shifting, as when Matulli turns into a bear, occurs in folk tales worldwide. Werewolves, the swan maidens of the ballet *Swan Lake*, and the selkies or seal people of Scottish legends are only some of the human/animal transformations found in folklore. One theory is that early man had to understand animals so closely – in order to hunt them, or to prevent them hunting him – that he thought himself into their minds, and then in fantasy into their bodies. Or perhaps the idea arose when a tribe, admiring the grace of the swan or the strength of the bear, adopted that animal as their totem and protector, and the people of the bear tribe eventually began to feel that they were bears. However it comes about, a character like Matulli, 'apt to take on the shape of an animal from time to time' (p. 11), is not at all unusual in folklore, and Mitchison uses the idea elsewhere: the young heroine of her novel *The Big House*, for instance, takes on the form of a swan.

Some passages in *Travel Light*, including the conversation between Steinvor and Halla on Dragon Mountain (pp. 29-33), are more easily understood with a little knowledge of the figures and concepts from Norse mythology listed below.

The Fenris Wolf, or Fenrir, is a fierce giant wolf, child of the evil god Loki. He is tied up with a magic chain, but at the Last Battle (see below) he will escape and kill Odin, before being killed himself.

The Last Battle, or Ragnarok, is the end of the world in Norse mythology. After the Fimbul Winter, three immensely harsh winters with no summers in between, the wolf Fenrir and the Midgard Serpent (see below) will break free and join giants and demons in a final battle against the gods. Odin will be killed and the earth will sink into the sea, but a new world, free of all wickedness and sadness, will take its place.

The Midgard Serpent is another child of Loki. To render it harmless Odin threw it into the ocean, but it has grown so big that it now coils round the whole world with its tail in its mouth. At the Last Battle it will kill the god Thor and be killed by him.

The Norns are three sisters, like the three Fates of Greek and Roman mythology, who control the destinies of gods and men. They tend the World Tree Yggdrasil (see below) and try to stop it decaying. In some accounts there are more than three Norns, and in others each person has his or her own Norn from the moment of birth.

Odin, sometimes called Woden or Wotan (Wednesday is Woden's Day), is the chief of the Norse gods, All-Father, father of gods and men. He is god of the dead, and presides in Valhalla (see below) over the banquets of those slain in battle. He is god of war, but also of wisdom, poetry and agriculture. He has only one eye, having given the other in exchange for a drink from the Well of Wisdom, by which he gained all knowledge. He goes about the world as the Wanderer, disguised in a blue cloak and slouch hat, with his ravens as messengers and advisers.

Valhalla is the hall in heaven to which heroes slain in battle are carried by the Valkyries (see below), to spend the rest of time feasting and carousing, until they are summoned to fight on the side of the gods in the Last Battle.

The Valkyries are warrior women who serve Odin. They ride into battle and select heroes destined to die. They carry them over Bifrost, the rainbow bridge, to Valhalla, and wait upon them at the everlasting banquet.

Yggdrasil, the World Tree, is a giant ash tree whose roots bind together heaven, earth and hell, and whose branches shelter all three worlds. Over the course of many ages even Yggdrasil will decay; the Norns, by tending it, try to slow up this process. At Ragnarok it will be burned up by the fire giant Surt.

5 Conclusion

The three short novels treated here have very little in common: they are (in broad terms) a historical novel, a children's book and a fantasy. Naomi Mitchison wrote other novels of all three kinds, and also science fiction, realistic novels, and a great deal of non-fiction for both adults and children. The diversity and wide range of her writing was a problem for critics throughout Mitchison's career. As a writer, and indeed as a person, she was impossible to pin down or pigeonhole.

Nevertheless the three books are comparable in some ways. Each, for instance, has something definite to say. *Early in Orcadia* sets out to show that all people share a common inheritance from our earliest ancestors. *The Big House* focuses more closely on the problem of social class, which has come about because people have forgotten or ignored that very fact. *Travel Light* upholds the value of the individual, the independent mind, against the mass movements of politics and war.

Each book also puts forward the proposal that human beings are not the only agents of progress and change. Mitchison never belonged to any church or followed any religious movement, and was often very dismissive of organised religion, but she clearly felt that there was – or should be – another dimension to life. From her books it seems that she was not sure what that dimension was – fairies, gods, or magical forces? – but she was convinced that it was there.

Mitchison was a prolific writer, but many of her books went quickly out of print, and though some have now been reprinted, the others are not easy to find. It is worth hunting for some of her collections of short stories; trying the humorous *Lobsters on the Agenda* or the Scottish historical novel *The Bull Calves*; or immersing yourself in the epic *The Corn King and the Spring Queen*. No two are alike. All offer lively, thoughtful writing driven by high intelligence and committed purpose. Diversity and depth: these are the hallmarks of Naomi Mitchison's work.

Bibliography

I: Selected works by Naomi Mitchison
The date of first publication is given in brackets. Details are then given of the most recent reprint or new edition. However, many of Naomi Mitchison's books are out of print, and are most likely to be found in libraries or second-hand bookshops.

a) Novels
The Corn King and the Spring Queen (1931). Canongate Classics, 2001.
The Bull Calves (1947). Virago, 1997.
The Big House (1950). Canongate Kelpies, 1987.
Travel Light (1952). Virago, 1985.
Lobsters on the Agenda (1952). House of Lochar, 1997.
Memoirs of a Spacewoman (1962). Women's Press, 1985.
Early in Orcadia (1987). House of Lochar, 2000.

b) Autobiography
Small Talk (1973).
All Change Here (1975).
Reprinted in one volume under title *As It Was*, Richard Drew, 1988.
You May Well Ask (1979). Collins Fontana, 1986.
Among You Taking Notes (1985). Phoenix Press, 2000.

II: Biography
Jill Benton, *Naomi Mitchison* (Pandora, 1990).
Jenni Calder, *The Nine Lives of Naomi Mitchison* (Virago, 1997).

III: Criticism
Julian D'Arcy, *Scottish Skalds and Sagamen* (Tuckwell Press, 1996).
Chapter 9 is on Mitchison and includes a discussion of *Travel Light*.
Jenni Calder, 'More than merely ourselves: Naomi Mitchison', *A History of Scottish Women's Writing*, ed. by Douglas Gifford and Dorothy McMillan (Edinburgh University Press, 1997), pp. 445-55.
An overview of Mitchison's life and work.
'Naomi Mitchison', *Scottish Writers Talking 2,* ed. by Isobel Murray (Tuckwell Press, 2002), pp. 67-109.
An interview which touches on *Early in Orcadia* and *The Big House*.